A Tribute to Oakdale

by

Samuel D. Bissette

CONTENTS

Introduction

Dedication

A Tribute to Oakdale

Bibliography

About the author

Appendix

Introduction

In the1980s I revived a previous interest in Wilmington's historic Oakdale Cemetery and began photographing its unusual markers and monuments, beautiful vistas, and bits of history on its thousands of gravestones. As time went on, I also filmed its changing beauty as the year's seasons progressed. The result was a large number of color slides of Oakdale. I recalled a program given at a Lions Club meeting years before by W. Kendall Dorsey who made a career of producing audiovisual presentations on North Carolina history. It seemed that a similar presentation on Oakdale would be a worthwhile project, and I could then put my slide collection to a good use. So *A Tribute to Oakdale* came into being. A sample viewing at the local Lions Club was well received, and other local organizations began to request similar showings for meeting programs. Eventually, I gave presentations to more than fifty local clubs, churches, and civic organizations. Once *A Tribute to Oakdale* had served its usefulness, I gave it to the New Hanover County Library.

In the fall of 2002 I completed a book, *From Inner Space to Outer Space,* intended for library and research use, in collaboration with Randall Library at the University of North Carolina at Wilmington. In reviewing the book with Andrew Dutka, special collections librarian at UNCW's Randall Library, I mentioned the existence of *A Tribute to Oakdale,* and it occurred to us that a conversion of the audiovisual format to book form would be worthwhile. As a result, I borrowed the presentation from the New Hanover County Library, began to convert the color slides into color prints, and developed the book format patterned after the previous book. Randall Library agreed to handle all matters pertaining to printing, production, and distribution. That is how this volume came into print.

This limited edition library research volume is being distributed, at no charge, by Randall Library to suitable libraries and other history-related institutions. Its pictures and text have been adapted into book form with as faithful a translation as practical. Unfortunately, the musical part of the original tape could not be incorporated into this volume. The appendix includes some important items pertaining to Oakdale that I thought would be of interest.

I am indebted to several persons and sources for their part in producing this volume: W. Kendall Dorsey (now deceased) for giving me the idea for the original presentation; Andrew Dutka, special collections librarian at Randall Library, for his help and encouragement; Ruby Raynor Bissette, my wife, for her support; Sabra Bissette Ledent, my daughter, for her editorial advice; Dr. David Bissette, my son, for acting as my computer consultant; Beverly Tetterton and the New Hanover County Library for their interest and assistance; Oakdale Cemetery Company for copyright permissions; and, especially, the William Madison Randall Library at the University of North Carolina at Wilmington for its years of interest and help in my art and history pursuits.

Samuel D. Bissette
January 30, 2003

Dedication

LOUIS TOOMER MOORE

This book is respectfully dedicated to Louis Toomer Moore who devoted himself to recording the history of the Lower Cape Fear Area. Especially, he loved Oakdale Cemetery and never tired of telling the story of this historic place to our citizens and visitors to Wilmington. He was an eminent historian, prominent businessman, veteran photographer and a distinguished gentleman. His biography may be found in the Appendix.

A TRIBUTE TO OAKDALE

The production of this volume
was made possible in part by the staff of
Special Collections at William Madison Randall Library,
University of North Carolina at Wilmington
Spring 2003

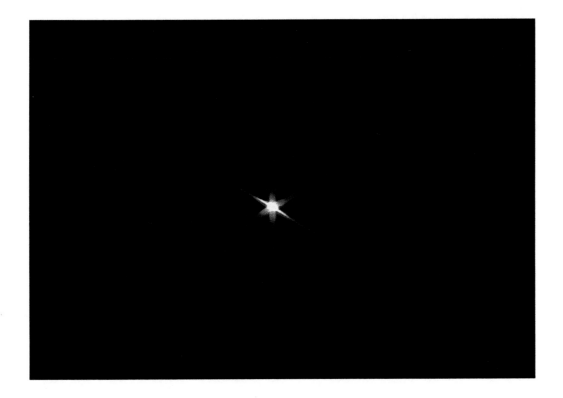

Since the beginning of recorded time, Man has been intrigued with the mysteries of the Universe, the Earth and himself. And, in all of the religions of present and past civilizations, there has been a search for the Creator of it all.

From an anthem sung in one of Wilmington's historic churches recently came these words:

When I gaze into the night skies and see the work of Your fingers, the moon and stars suspended in space; What is Man, that You are mindful of him?

This is a story about Man, Time and Eternity; a city and its people; and a special place of beauty and history within that city. Man has found that our Universe, the Sun and the Moon, plants and living creatures, Earth's seasons aand civilizations run in cycles, just as Man's life itself - creation, maturity, decline and death and, yes, a new life after death.

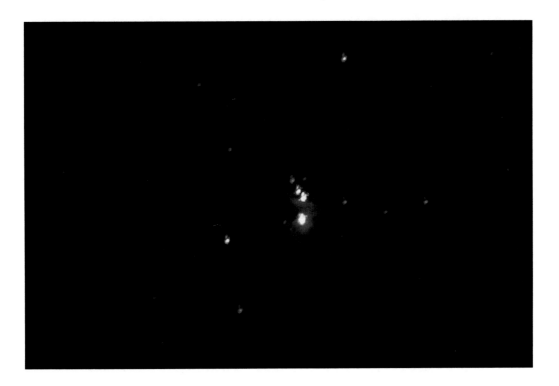

This story deals with that part of life on Earth, and especially that part about death. The city of which I speak is Wilmington, North Carolina and its people, the Wilmingtonians of the past.

The place within that city is Oakdale Cemetery.

And this story is a tribute to Oakdale.

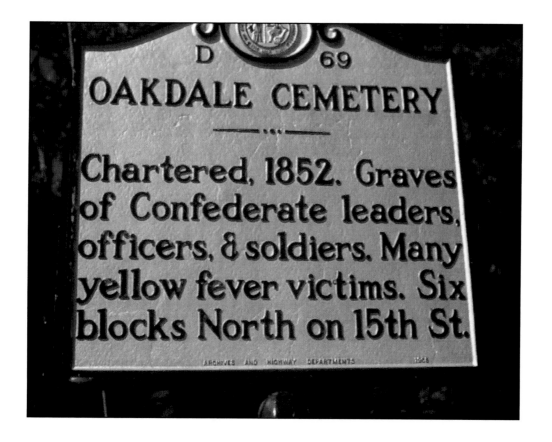

At the corner of Fifteenth and Market Streets in Wilmington, there is a seldom-noticed North Carolina Historical Marker entitled "Oakdale Cemetery". Found at the northern end of Fifteenth Street, Oakdale is a unique landmark founded in 1852 and is a place of scenic beauty and historical interest covering 165 acres.

Its beauty is created by its abundance of white dogwood and giant oak trees, azaleas and camellias and magnolias, its shady lanes, and many memorials of granite and marble.

It is a record of history and genealogy with its mausoleums,
monuments and markers with their inscriptions.

It is also a record of love, respect, commemoration, and remembrance for the more than twenty thousand Wilmington citizens who have found their last resting place in Oakdale.

We are now ready to take a short visual trip through this unusual place noting the many things that it can tell us about Wilmington's past and realizing that they can only be a small sample of what there is to be seen here.

First. let us visit the seasons of the year in Oakdale......

Spring......

Summer......

And the golds of Autumn arrive......

Autumn......

Winter......

......and the Christmas Season......

......have given us a sampling of Nature's beauty.

Now let us see some of the beauty created by Man to be found at
Oakdale. (above and on the following two pages)

The beauty of the sculptures in marble, ornate inscriptions, unique memorial markers, stained glass and massive mausoleums are principally found in the older area just within the entrance gate.

Other areas of the cemetery reveal simpler forms of monuments and markers.

Historically, many events are intertwined with the lives of the people of Wilmington, but none more than the wars of our country since Oakdale's creation - The War between the States, War of 1898, World Wars I and II, Korean and Vietnam.

The Civil War of 1861-1865 left its mark heavily in Oakdale. An obscure underground tomb with a covered entrance is the burying place for fourteen Confederate soldiers.

In an elevated and enclosed area in the west side of the cemetery is found The Confederate Memorial created through the efforts of the Ladies Memorial Association with a land gift from Oakdale. Here lie the remains of three hundred thirty-five soldiers re-interred from other areas of the cemetery.

ERECTED TO THE MEMORY OF
CHARLES QUIGLEY
FIRST SUPERINTENDENT OF
OAKDALE CEMETERY
HAVING SERVED FROM
NOV. 6, 1855
UNTIL HIS DEATH DURING THE
YELLOW FEVER EPIDEMIC
OCT. 1862

In 1862 a major calamity fell upon Wilmington when it lost nearly one-third of its two thousand population in an epidemic of yellow fever. Thought to be brought into the city from the packet "Kate", it spread like wildfire among the populace striking down hundreds as it raged.

Many markers bear death dates from this peiod, including one doctor and two ministers buried here and one buried elsewhere. While tirelessly serving his fellow men, Reverend Robert B. Drane, rector of Saint James Episcopal Church, and Reverend John L. Prichard, pastor of First Baptist Church, died of yellow fever and are buried here, and Reverend Father Thomas Murphy, pastor of Saint Thomas Catholic Church, is buried beneath the walls of his beloved church.

In a common grave area a few hundred feet within the entrance, hundreds of yellow fever victims were buried in rows marked by numbered stones, or in a common grave.

Four of Wilmington's Confederate generals, and other officers, have their graves in
Oakdale.

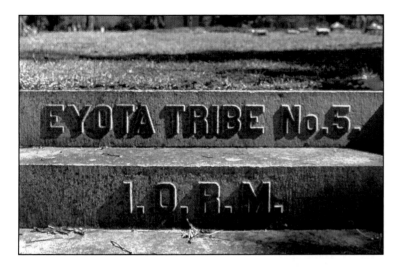

Located within the cemetery, in addition to the Confederate and yellow fever areas, are several special areas - some for large families, fraternal orders, the Hebrew Cemetery, the Young Men's Christian Association, and a number of others.

NORTH CAROLINA'S
FIRST ELECTED GOVERNOR
EDWARD BISHOP DUDLEY
BORN DECEMBER 15, 1789.
DIED OCTOBER 30, 1855.

Another is an historical area marked by the graves of Edward B. Dudley,
first elected governor of North Carolina; ......

......Henry Bacon, architect of the Lincoln Memorial; and other notable persons.

I would like to comment on a few of the many people who left their mark in history that are interred here. Mrs. Rose O'Neal Greenhow, Confederate secret service agent, who was drowned while running the blockade at Fort Fisher in September, 1864.

Mr. Pembroke Jones, prominent philanthropist, whose mausoleum is found
in the circular historical area.

Mr. James Walker, whose name was perpetuated in the name of James Walker Memorial Hospital, predecessor to New Hanover Memorial Hospital. His grave monument bears this inscription: "After a frugal and industrious life, he left to the afflicted and suffering a lasting memorial of his beneficence in yonder hospital which bears his honoured name".

Reverend Andrew J. Howell, author of the "Book of Wilmington".

Mr. Arthur Bluethenthal, a brave and highly esteemed young Jewish man, who was shot down during World War I while flying with the Lafayette Flying Corps, with his name being given to Bluethenthal Field, now also called New Hanover County Airport.

In 1855, six year old Annie DeRossett, daughter of the first president of Oakdale Dr. A. J. DeRossett, Jr., died and became the first person to be interred in the new cemetery. Her gravestone simply states "Our Little Annie".

Mr. Harry Meyer Solomon, a distinguished Wilmingtonian, for whom Solomon
Towers was named and head of the seventy man steering committee created to plan
New Hanover Memorial Hospital.

Mr. Lewis Philip Hall, author of "Land of the Golden River".

Captain John Newland Maffitt on whose gravestone is inscribed: "Entered service U.S. Navy 1832 at age of thirteen. Commander U.S. Navy from 1849 to April 1861. Resigned U.S. Navy April 1861. Entered Confederate States Navy May 13, 1861. Served as Captain until 1865".

There are many others worthy of mention and their omission is not intended as any lack of respect.

Scattered throughout the older section are monuments indicating that persons were not native to America and stating their birthplace.

Some of these indicate England, Scotland, Ireland, Germany and other countries of Europe, pointing up the fact of America being the great melting pot of the world populated with immigrants from other countries.

KATHERYN SHAW TUCKER PEEBLES
1908 —— 1972
A SPECIAL LADY
WHO FOUND FAULT WITH NO ONE

A visit to Oakdale would not be complete without lingering over the many epitaphs that denote words of remembrance, love, respect and praise of the persons interred. (continued over the six pages that follow)

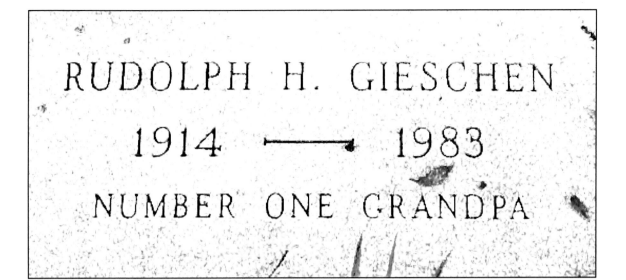

RUDOLPH H. GIESCHEN
1914 ———→ 1983
NUMBER ONE GRANDPA

DOROTHY WYSONG
GIESCHEN
JAN. 17, 1917   SEP. 21, 1987
"MAMA DOT"

WILLIE POISSON MONROE
AUGUST 25, 1867
JANUARY 27, 1932

HE HAS ANSWERED THE LAST ALARM

There are many family names found in Oakdale that represent many generations, some going back to well before the Revolutionary War. One finds a number of these perpetuated in the names of streets and parks, on dedication plates for public buildings, names of schools and buildings, and in other ways. (continued over the three pages that follow)

53

HUGH MACRAE

MARCH 30, 1865

OCTOBER 20, 1951

"HE MAKETH ME TO LIE DOWN
IN GREEN PASTURES."

A century ago, the mortality rate of little children was very high from diseases that had no cure, as well as childhood accidents. A very sad example of this is to be found in the Gause family plot. Five little children, the eldest having reached only five years of age, were taken from this family by death. On the monument, with the name of the mother, Sarah Gause, is shown the record of the passing of the little childen, as follows, separate identical stones also marking the individual graves. Mary Jeffords, born July 18, 1834 - died May 25, 1835 - - - - Benjamin, born April 22, 1840 - died Sept. 11, 1843 - - - - Martha Judith, born Sept. 14, 1838 - died Sept 14, 1843 - - - - John Benjamin, born Sept 24, 1843 - died May 19, 1846 - - - - Mary Dumont, born Feb. 4, 1842 - died Sept. 13, 1843. Then follows the sad line "The above five children lie by their Mother". Please note that three of these died from Sept. 11th to the 14th, 1843.

Unusual circumstances are recorded on the marble monument of Lizzie B. Turlington, who was born on December 10, 1862 according to the face of the stone, with this inscription on the side: "Murdered by W. L. Bingham on December 17, 1886, Age 24 years & 7 days".

Doctor William Crawford Willkings was slain in a duel in 1856, stemming from a local political election. He is believed to be the last man killed in the South in a political duel.

On a Sunday afternoon, in the nineteen fifties, my friend Louis Toomer Moore, an eminent historian, gave my family a tour of Oakdale Cemetery, acquainting us with his extensive knowledge and stories about the cemetery. I am deeply indebted to him for creating my interest in Oakdale, and for providing much of the information from which this brief presentation was prepared. His history of Oakdale, first written in 1955 for his book "Stories Old and New of the Cape Fear Region" and reroduced later by by Oakdale, is a well-written and fact-filled documentary of Oakdale. We citizens of Wilmington owe him a debt of gratitude for his fine record.

My thanks also to Robert Coleman, former caretaker, for his conducted tour in 1988......

...... and to the several fine authors of the Cape Fear Area whose works provided valuable background.

I hope this brief visit has been worthwhile to you......

......and is helpful in giving an appreciation of the history, people and traditions of the fine city of Wilmington, which celebrates its 250th birthday in 1989.

And, let us particularly remember those people of the past who have left us the legacy of a fine historic city,......

......which I hope we have preserved and bettered with our love, care and work while our lives were lived here,......

......and that we may have fulfilled the words of the poet who said, "and departing, leave behind us footprints on the sands of time".

Bibliography

"Armchair Astronomy."*The International Tape and Cine Society* (England). December 1995.

"The Astromicroscopic Universe of Sam Bissette." *The Practical Observer* (New Jersey). 6, no. 4 (1996).

Bissette, Samuel D. "A Guide to Astromicroscopy." *The Reflector* (Astronomical League of the U.S.). May 1994.

———. *A Guide to Astromicroscopy.* Wilmington, N.C.: Cape Fear Astronomical Society, 1994.

———. *An Astromicroscopy Study of the Southern Hemisphere.* Wilmington, N.C.: Cape Fear Astronomical Society, 1995.

Brock, Mary Anne Browder. "Sam Bissette's Universe." *UNCW Magazine* (University of North Carolina at Wilmington). 1983 (article and front cover).

Brown, David. *North Carolina: New Directions For An Old Land.* Northridge, California. Windsor Publications. 1986 (nine watercolor illustrations in text, endpapers, and dedication page).

Carr, Genie. "An Artist's Brush and Palette Replaced His Business Desk." *Winston-Salem Journal,* March 9, 1986.

Cashman, Diane. *Cape Fear Adventure.* Woodland Hills, Calif.: Windsor Publications. 1983 (front cover illustration).

Julian, Dennis M. "Sam Bissette Paints North Carolina Beauty for Wachovia." *North Carolina* (magazine, Raleigh, N.C.). June 1977.

Mills, Beverly. "Artwork Goes Over Big in Wilmington." *News and Observer* (Raleigh, N.C.), October 21, 1979.

Nadeau, Nola, "Bissette Watercolors Translated in Mosaics." *Wilmington Star-News* (Wilmington, N.C.), June 14, 1979.

N. C. People, a program of the University of North Carolina Television Network PBS. Interview with Dr. Bill Friday, President of UNC, August 1985.

"NORTH CAROLINA—Circa 1900." *The State* (Raleigh, N.C.), August 1984 (front cover and article).

Roberts, Lee. "A New View of the Universe." *Wilmington Star-News* (Wilmington, N.C.), April 24, 1994.

———. "Watercolors Show State's Past." *Wilmington Star-News* (Wilmington, N.C.), December 2, 1984,

"Samuel D. Bissette," *American Artist.* March 1984

Steelman, Ben. "Retiree Turns His Hobby into Second Career in Art." *Wilmington Star-News* (Wilmington, N.C.), July 27, 1983.

"The Story of Sam Bissette's Unique Voyage in Art And Astronomy". *The Practical Observer* (New Jersey). 7, no. 2 (1997).

"Vignettes of AWS People: Samuel D. Bissette." *American Watercolor Society Newsletter.* Summer 1985.

"Wachovia Sponsoring Watercolor Art Depicting Old Days in North Carolina." *American Banker.* August 1984.

Who's Who in American Art, (Bowker), various editions beginning in 1982.

Who's Who in the South and Southwest, Who's Who in America, Who's Who in the World, Who's Who in American Art (Marquis), various editions beginning in 1982.

About the Author

Samuel D. Bissette was born in 1921 in Wilson, North Carolina and has lived in Wilmington since 1936. He and his wife Ruby were married in 1943 and have a son and daughter and two grandchildren. Following high school and military service of three years in World War II, he commenced a fifty-year career in banking. At age fifty, he became interested in art, sought professional instruction, and began a thirty year career in art overlapping his banking responsibilities. In 2002 his body of original artworks number more than fifteen hundred and are located in nearly all of the states in the United States and a number of countries abroad. He has exhibited widely in one-man exhibitions throughout North Carolina and shown in Washington and New York. He is an original trustee of the N.C. Museum of Art and past president of Saint John's Museum of Art in Wilmington.

In 1990, he became interested in astronomy, procured the proper equipment and began a concentrated period of observing and astrophotography. Visits were made to a number of observatories and astronomical installations over the United States and some abroad in the search for knowledge. In 1994, he originated an unconventional method of astronomical observing and named it astromicroscopy. It is now in use throughout the world after national acceptance by the Astronomical League of the United States in 1995. Combining art with astronomy, he completed a sixty painting exhibition *The Universe According to Earth* and gave it to the University of North Carolina at Wilmington where it is on permanent exhibition in their new science building,. Several research projects were completed resulting in two books on astromicroscopy available on the Internet and at various libraries.

Since age eleven, he has been an amateur photographer. This has been an asset in securing art material on field trips in this country and abroad. An interest in microscope photography resulted in research in this field. Combining art with photomicrography, he then produced *Images from the Microworld*, a thirty-four piece exhibition and gave it to UNCW where it is on permanent display in their original science building.

A lifelong interest in history has resulted in a number of history projects which are detailed in the preceding chapters. Additional information is available in libraries at UNCW, New Hanover County, and local historical societies. The Internet is also an excellent source of information.

Appendix

There are three documents in this section that relate to Oakdale Cemetery. The first page describes *A Tribute to Oakdale*, the audio-film presentation. The second page relates its showings in the New Hanover County area. The last document, consisting of seven pages, is an excerpt from the booklet published in 1991 by the Oakdale Cemetery Company with the title of *A Tribute to Oakdale*. The last page is a biography of Louis T. Moore.

A TRIBUTE TO OAKDALE

The above is a photograph of the audio-visual presentation that I made in 1989. It consists of 128 color slides in the tray, a 21 minute audio cassette, and a manuscript. When it is shown, the audio tape is played on a cassette tape player and the slides are projected on a projection screen in coordination with the audio narration. A manuscript is being viewed simultaneously to guide the operator. During 1990 and 1991 more than 50 showings were made to about 2,000 people in the Wilmington area. A partial listing of these may be found on the following page.

GROUPS TO WHICH *A TRIBUTE TO OAKDALE* WAS SHOWN IN 1990-1991

Oakdale Board of Trustees
Latimer House docents
Cape Fear Astronomical Society
New Hanover County Museum
North Carolina Sorosis – night
North Carolina Sorosis – day
PEO – a sisterhood
Cape Fear Contractor's Association
Winter Park Seniors Group
Saint Mathews Church elders
Wesley Memorial Church Men's Group
New Horizons School
Noble Middle School
Baptist Hill Sunday School Class
First Baptist Church group
Rotary Club – Wilmington
Rotary Club – East
Rotary Club – Cape Fear
Optimist Club
Lions Club
Kiwanis Club
Civitan Club
Encore Club
First Presbyterian Church
First Christian Church
Plantation Village
Oakdale publicity people
Engineer's Club
Saint John's Episcopal Church
Broadfoot, Bridgers, Taylor
Lower Cape Fear Historical Society
University Adult Scholars luncheon
Cornelia Nixon Davis Nursing Home
Saint Anne's Guild, Saint James Episcopal Church
Winter Park School third grade
Pine Valley Methodist Church
Catherine Kennedy Home
Wilmington Exchange Club
Colonial Dames
Tuesday Morning Book Club
Three First Baptist Church circles

A Tribute
to
Oakdale

1852–1991

Front cover of Oakdale Cemetery Company's booklet published in 1991

— PREFACE —

In 1990, the Oakdale Cemetery Board of Directors undertook a capital fund drive to pay for critical repairs to the cemetery grounds and other needs. Of particular importance was a new irrigation system, new paving for driveways, security fencing, office building, and land clearing for grave site expansion.

In addition, it was decided to publish an updated version of "Beautiful Oakdale," a story written by Louis Toomer Moore in 1955, describing Oakdale's interesting history, listing many of the prominent people interred there, and recording unusual events surrounding the lives and deaths of many others. Upon hearing about the Oakdale Cemetery Restoration Fund and its purposes, a grandson of Mr. Moore, Louis Moore Bacon, generously contributed the funds for the production of this booklet.

Tom Broadfoot and Rickie Broadfoot, of Broadfoot Publishing Company, designed and provided the layout for its printing, and Sabra Bissette Ledent edited the text. For the color photographs and additional text material taken from his outstanding audio-visual presentation on Oakdale, we are indebted to Samuel D. Bissette.

Finally, to the many people whose efforts made the fund drive successful and to those who contributed financially, the board of Directors is most grateful.

Kenneth M. Sprunt, *President*
Lawrence C. Rose, *Vice President*
Willie Mae Shawver, *Secretary*
William E. Perdew, *Treasurer*
Harold D. Alexius, *Director*

James D. Carr, *Director*
Lenox G. Cooper, Jr., *Director*
Catherine Solomon, *Director*
John T. Talbert, *Director*
C. Heide Trask, Jr., *Director*

FRONT GATE OF THE CEMETERY

A Brief History

At the corner of Fifteenth and Market streets in Wilmington, North Carolina, stands a North Carolina historical marker entitled "Oakdale Cemetery." Found one-half mile to the north at the end of Fifteenth Street, Oakdale is a unique landmark, first planned in 1852. It is a place of scenic beauty and historical interest covering 165 acres. Oakdale's beauty is created by its abundance of white dogwood and giant oak trees, its azaleas and camellias and magnolias, its shady lanes, and its many memorials of granite and marble. It is a record of history and genealogy with its inscribed mausoleums, monuments, and markers. It is also a record of love, respect, commemoration, and remembrance for the more than twenty-two thousand Wilmington citizens who have found their last resting place in Oakdale.

Possibly, there is no other cemetery in North Carolina—or for that matter in the entire South—which contains within its boundaries the graves of so many famous men and women who have had a direct and marked influence on the recorded history of the United States. If the stones that mark the resting places of these distinguished persons could offer an oral recital of valiant deeds and splendid services, the story unfolded would be heard

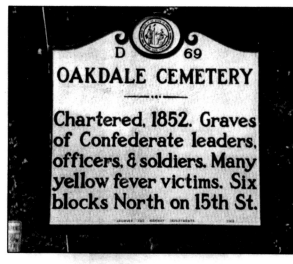

with amazement and pride by the modern visitor.

The origins of Oakdale go back to the mid-nineteenth century when the old time-honored custom of interments within town churchyards was fast disappearing. Gradually, it was being supplanted with the cemetery system of burials. Because of their relationship to civic health, burials had been one of vital concern to citizens for years past. In early 1852, several prominent businessmen of Wilmington met at the Commissioners' Hall (then on the second floor of the old so-called Mud Market, at Second and Market Streets) to discuss the subject of a new cemetery, to be located somewhere beyond the town limits. After a full discussion, a committee was appointed consisting of the following gentlemen: Dr. A. J. deRosset, Jr., Edward Kidder, O. G. Parsley, Col. John MacRae, Capt. Charles E. Ellis, S. D. Wallace, and Dougald MacMillan. It was their duty to select a site for the company, under the corporate name of "The Proprietors of the Wilmington Cemetery."

The members of the committee gave their first attention to a charter which was granted by the General Assembly of North Carolina and ratified on December 27, 1852. A search for a site for the cemetery followed, and a "Neck of Land" on the east side of "Burnt Mill" Creek was chosen. This area was northeast of the limits of the town proper and there Oakdale Cemetery was located. Nature seemed to have molded the ground for that purpose and left it for many to beautify. Over the years this has been done in a way that has made the reservation one of the loveliest and most impressive found in the South.

On November 16, 1853, the committee met, and John A. Taylor was appointed chairman and Mauger London secretary. The chairman stated that the meeting was called to organize the company by the election of a president and six directors to serve until the time of the regular annual meeting on the second Monday

in January 1854. The election was held and resulted in the drafting of Dr. deRosset, as president, and Edward Kidder, James Cassidey, John A. Taylor, Henry Nutt, William A. Wright, and George R. French as directors.

Since that day in 1853, management has remained vested in a board of directors who, through the succeeding decades, has rendered faithful, conscientious, and devoted service, without expectation of remuneration or reward. Ownership of a lot, however, is required to be eligible for membership on the board. This is a wise and provident factor, assuring sympathetic and considerate attention by board members to the countless questions and problems that present themselves. Under the democratic policy that has always prevailed, annual elections are held, and lot owners are given an opportunity to signify their wishes about the Board's membership.

The new board held its first meeting on November 25, 1853, and elected J. T. Munds secretary and treasurer. The committee on the site for the cemetery and the charter for the company reported that it had performed its duty.

The sixty-five acre site for the cemetery had been agreed upon and paid for, the purchase price being $1,100. The committee offered to turn it over to the company for the same amount. The offer was accepted, and the amount involved was to be paid to the committee from the first funds collected. At a subsequent meeting the secretary and treasurer reported the deed in hand and paid for. The transfer deed to the company is dated April 8, 1854.

With such an intelligent and far-sighted board of directors to push matters to completion, delay certainly was not the rule. There was plenty of work to do before the grounds could be prepared for the sale of lots. They began at once under their own supervision and assisted by Charles Quigley, the first super-

WIDE MARL WALKS OF 1890S

—3—

intendent. Mr. Quigley was a victim of the terrible yellow fever epidemic of 1862. The grounds were surveyed by L. Turner, and Sections A, B, C, D, E, F, G, and H were laid out. A map was made and accepted by the directors as the official plan for those sections.

On December 5, 1854, lots in the particular sections named were ordered sold by M. Cronly, a prominent citizen. A minimum of $50 was placed on each lot. At this sale nearly every lot was bought at a premium, ranging from $60 to $90 for each lot.

Following the sale of lots, the cemetery was declared ready for interments. This was followed with an ordinance, passed by the Commissioners forbidding interments within the limits of the town.

It seems sadly ironic that the first burial in Oakdale Cemetery on the 5th of February, 1855, was that of little Annie deRosset, aged six years, the young daughter of the president, Dr. deRosset. Her gravestone simply states, "Our Little Annie."

In more recent years, conforming with modern trends and ideas, two important changes in general policy were effected. The first was the Annex Extension, dedicated in 1945, and the second was the Memorial Garden, made available to the public in 1950. The Memorial Garden consists of garden areas and flat bronze memorials which are in general symmetrical conformity. Within the original lovely and spacious outlines of Oakdale, there are now approximately 135 acres, and in the two new sections just described, about 30 additional acres.

ANNIE DeROSSET, FIRST INTERMENT
AT OAKDALE IN 1855

LOUIS T. MOORE
1885 – 1961

Mr. Moore was born in Wilmington on May 17, 1885, the son of Col. Roger Moore and Eugenia Beery Moore. He was a direct descendent of "King" Roger Moore, who built Orton plantation in 1725. Mr. Moore married the former Florence Hill Kidder and had three daughters— Mrs. John O. Dunn, Mrs. William E. Perdew, and Mrs. Zack Bacon, Jr. Members of the family have been prominent in Southeastern North Carolina for generations.

After attending public schools in Wilmington, Mr. Moore graduated from the University of North Carolina in 1906. There he was a catcher on the baseball team, a member of Kappa Alpha fraternity, and on the staff of the student newspaper, the *Tar Heel*.

In July 1906, he joined the staff of the *Wilmington Dispatch*, now the *Morning Star*, as a reporter. Later he became city editor. In 1913, he left newspaper work and went into business as part owner of the Davis Moore Paint Company.

In 1921, James H. Cowan resigned as secretary of the Chamber of Commerce to become mayor of Wilmington, and Mr. Moore was selected to succeed him. He served as secretary for the next twenty years. Two major projects of the Chamber during those years were constant advocacy of a deeper channel in the Cape Fear River and extension of the inland waterway.

During the years he was secretary of the Chamber, Mr. Moore's interest in history grew. He was extremely active in encouraging the state, through its Department of Archives and History and Highway Commission, to erect historical markers in Wilmington and vicinity.

He became chairman of the New Hanover Historical Commission in 1947. In recognition of his distinguished work in historical preservation and restoration, he received the Charles A. Cannon award in 1960 from the North Carolina Society for the Preservation of Antiquities.

Mr. Moore wrote innumerable historical articles for state, southern and national newspapers and magazines. He was considered one of the outstanding authorities on the history of the Lower Cape Fear region.

During his more active years, he was secretary of the Wilmington Rotary Club for a decade and was awarded the Rotary civic service gold pin for general community service. He also was chairman of the County Board of Elections, president of the North Carolina Commercial Secretaries Association and Chairman of the two-hundredth anniversary pageant commemorating Wilmington's founding.

He was a life-long member of Grace Methodist Church.